W9-CND-950

What Lives in the Tundra?

Oona Gaarder-Juntti

Consulting Editor, Diane Craig, M.A./Reading Specialist

Published by ABDO Publishing Company, 8000 West 78th Street, Edina, Minnesota 55439. Copyright © 2009 by Abdo Consulting Group, Inc. International copyrights reserved in all countries. No part of this book may be reproduced in any form without written permission from the publisher. Super SandCastle™ is a trademark and logo of ABDO Publishing Company.

Printed in the United States.

Credits
Editor: Liz Salzmann
Content Developer: Nancy Tuminelly
Cover and Interior Design and Production: Oona Gaarder-Juntti, Mighty Media
Illustration: Oona Gaarder-Juntti
Photo Credits: AbleStock, Creatas, iStockphoto/Tomo Jesenicnik/Frank Leung/ Serdar Uckun, ShutterStock

Library of Congress Cataloging-in-Publication Data

Gaarder-Juntti, Oona, 1979-

What lives in the tundra? / Oona Gaarder-Juntti.

p. cm. -- (Animal habitats)

ISBN 978-1-60453-179-4

1. Tundra animals--Juvenile literature. 2. Mountain animals--Juvenile literature. I. Title.

QL113.G24 2009

591.75'86--dc22

2008005481

Super SandCastle™ books are created by a team of professional educators, reading specialists, and content developers around five essential components—phonemic awareness, phonics, vocabulary, text comprehension, and fluency—to assist young readers as they develop reading skills and strategies and increase their general knowledge. All books are written, reviewed, and leveled for guided reading, early reading intervention, and Accelerated Reader® programs for use in shared, guided, and independent reading and writing activities to support a balanced approach to literacy instruction.

About SUPER SANDCASTLE™

Bigger Books for Emerging Readers
Grades K–4

Created for library, classroom, and at-home use, Super SandCastle™ books support and engage young readers as they develop and build literacy skills and will increase their general knowledge about the world around them. Super SandCastle™ books are part of SandCastle™, the leading PreK–3 imprint for emerging and beginning readers. Super SandCastle™ features a larger trim size for more reading fun.

Let Us Know
Super SandCastle™ would like to hear your stories about reading this book. What was your favorite page? Was there something hard that you needed help with? Share the ups and downs of learning to read. We want to hear from you! Send us an e-mail.

sandcastle@abdopublishing.com

Contact us for a complete list of SandCastle™, Super SandCastle™, and other nonfiction and fiction titles from ABDO Publishing Company.

www.abdopublishing.com • 8000 West 78th Street Edina, MN 55439 • 800-800-1312 • 952-831-1632 fax

Alpine tundras are located on the tops of tall mountains. The alpine tundra begins where trees stop growing.

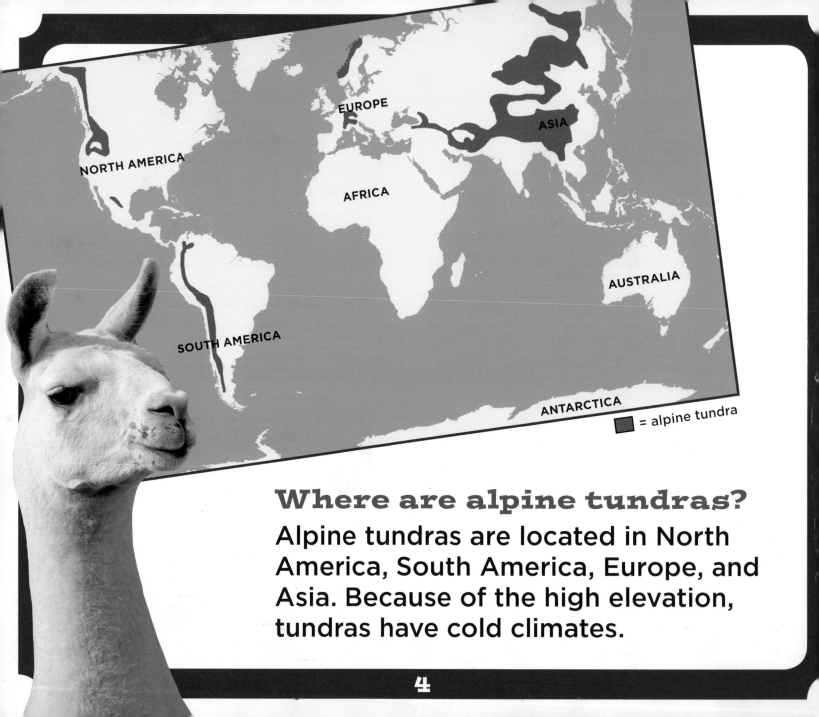

Where are alpine tundras?

Alpine tundras are located in North America, South America, Europe, and Asia. Because of the high elevation, tundras have cold climates.

What does the alpine tundra look like?

Alpine tundras are rocky with no trees. Each tundra has different animals that have adapted to living there. The tundra of Rocky Mountain National Park is home to elk, bighorn sheep, and marmots.

PIKA

Animal class: Mammal
Location: North America, Eastern Europe, and Asia

Pikas are related to rabbits. Some pikas live in piles of rock. Other pikas dig burrows in the ground. Pikas are very vocal. They call and whistle to each other.

Pikas gather grass and make haypiles for food during the winter.

Yellow-Bellied Marmot

Animal class: **Mammal**
Location: **North America**

Yellow-bellied marmots eat grasses, flowers, fruits, insects, and grains. They dig burrows under rocks to keep out predators. During the winter they hibernate in their burrows.

In the summer, yellow-bellied marmots spend a lot of time sunbathing.

Andean Condor

Animal class: Bird
Location: South America

Andean condors are the largest flying birds in South America. They fly long distances looking for food. They are scavengers that find and eat dead animals.

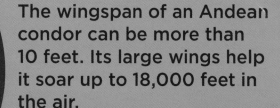

The wingspan of an Andean condor can be more than 10 feet. Its large wings help it soar up to 18,000 feet in the air.

ALPINE IBEX

Animal class: Mammal
Location: Europe

Alpine ibexes are wild goats. They live in a mountain range called the Alps. Ibexes eat grass, moss, flowers, leaves, and twigs.

Male ibexes have horns that can be up to 55 inches long.

BIGHORN SHEEP

Animal class: Mammal
Location: North America

Male bighorn sheep are called rams. Rams have large curved horns. They have head-butting contests to decide who will be the leader.

Bighorn sheep have thick skulls to keep them from getting badly hurt.

14

ELK

Animal class: Mammal
Location: North America

Elk are the second largest species of deer in the world. Male elk have antlers that fall off each winter and grow back in the spring. Elk are also called wapiti.

Elk live together in large herds in the winter. They form smaller herds in the summer.

17

SNOW LEOPARD

Animal class: Mammal
Location: Central Asia

The snow leopard has thick fur and wide, furry feet that act like snowshoes. It also has powerful back legs. A snow leopard can leap as far as 50 feet to catch prey.

The snow leopard has a long tail that helps it balance on rocky cliffs. Its tail can be more than three feet long.

GRIZZLY BEAR

Animal class: Mammal
Location: North America

Grizzly bears can be eight feet long and weigh more than 800 pounds. Each grizzly bear digs its own den to hibernate in during the winter.

Grizzly bears eat a lot during the summer and fall. They store fat on their bodies that they live off of while they are hibernating.

Have you ever been to an alpine tundra?

More Alpine Tundra Animals

Can you learn about these alpine tundra animals?

alpaca

black bear

caribou

chamois

chinchilla

ermine

grasshopper

gyrfalcon

llama

lynx

moose

mountain goat

red fox

snowshoe hare

vicuña

vole

willow ptarmigan

wolf

wolverine

yak

Glossary

adapt – to change in order to function better for a specific need or situation.

burrow – a hole or tunnel dug in the ground by a small animal for use as shelter.

climate – the usual weather in a place.

elevation – how high something is.

hibernate – to pass the winter in a deep sleep.

mammal – a warm-blooded animal that has hair and whose females produce milk to feed the young.

prey – an animal that is hunted or caught for food.

related – having a relationship or connection.

scavenger – one that feeds on whatever garbage or dead animals it finds.

skull – the bones that protect the brain and form the face.

soar – to fly high in the air.

species – a group of related living beings.

vocal – using the voice to make sounds or communicate.

wingspan – the distance from one wing tip to the other when the wings are fully spread.